Fact Finders®

Questions and Answers: Countries

Kenya

A Question and Answer Book

Revised Edition

by Sara Louise Kras

Consultant:
Dr. David Sandgren
Professor of History
Concordia College
Moorhead, Minnesota

CAPSTONE PRESS
a capstone imprint

Fact Finders is published by Capstone Press
1710 Roe Crest Drive, North Mankato, Minnesota 56003
www.mycapstone.com

Library of Congress Cataloging-in-Publication Data is available on the Library of Congress website.
ISBN 978–1-5157-5851-8 (revised paperback)
ISBN 978-1-5157-5856-3 (ebook)

Editorial Credits
Silver Editions, editorial, design, photo research and production; Kia Adams, set designer;
Maps.com, cartographer

Photo Credits
Alamy: Images of Africa Photobank, 23; ASSOCIATED PRESS, 9; Getty Images: Ed Lacey/
Popperfoto, 19, Nigel Pavitt, 12; iStockphoto: Britta Kasholm-Tengve, Cover, 27, jacobeukman,
11, ranplett, 15; Newscom: Everett Collection, 7; Shutterstock: Aleksandar Todorovic, 25,
Byelikova Oksana, 4, Dawn Hudson, bottom 29, Eduard Kyslynskyy, 21, IndustryAndTravel,
13, Juliya Shangarey, 16, Maciej Bledowski, top 29, Matej Kastelic, 1, meunierd, 17

Printed in the United States of America.
009913R

Table of Contents

Features

Where is Kenya?

Kenya is a country in eastern Africa. It is about the size of the U.S. state of Texas.

Kenya has many kinds of landforms. Sandy beaches line the coast along the Indian Ocean. North of the coast are grasslands called **savannas**. In the north is the Chalbi desert. Mountains and plateaus rise up in the west. They include Mount Kenya, the highest point in the country. The Great Rift Valley splits the highlands.

Kenya's savannas support a great deal of wildlife, including giraffes and zebras.

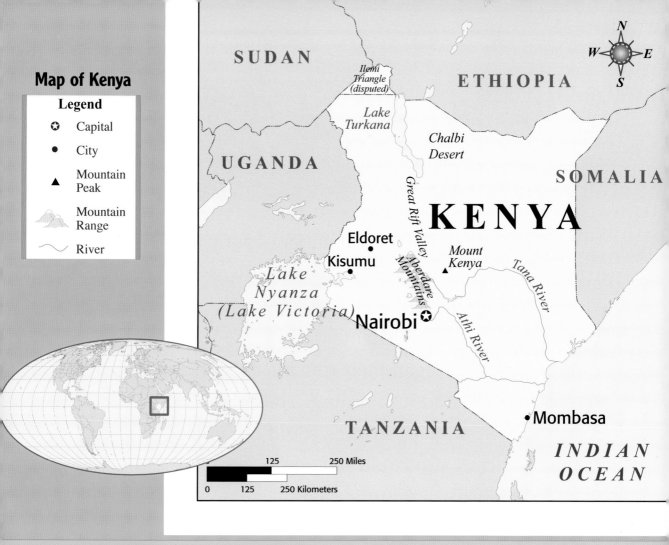

Map of Kenya

Legend

✪ Capital

● City

▲ Mountain Peak

⛰ Mountain Range

〰 River

SUDAN

ETHIOPIA

Ilemi Triangle (disputed)

Lake Turkana

Chalbi Desert

SOMALIA

UGANDA

Great Rift Valley

KENYA

Eldoret

Mount Kenya ▲

Tana River

Kisumu

Aberdare Mountains

Lake Nyanza (Lake Victoria)

Nairobi ✪

Athi River

TANZANIA

● Mombasa

INDIAN OCEAN

125   250 Miles

0   125   250 Kilometers

Kenya's location on the equator makes the country warm. Kenya's desert lands in the north are the driest areas. The savannas are also dry but receive more rain than deserts. The highlands receive the most rainfall.

When did Kenya become a country?

Kenya became an independent country on December 12, 1963. Before that, it was governed by the United Kingdom (UK), often referred to as Britain.

The British began their rule in 1895. They took the best land for farming. The British passed laws so that Africans could not own land. Africans also could not vote.

In the 1940s, a group called the Kikuyu objected to these laws. They joined with other Africans to challenge and fight the British. Many Africans were jailed or killed.

Fact!

Jomo Kenyatta was a leader of the Africans challenging British rule. He was jailed for eight years for his ideas and actions.

After being in prison, Jomo Kenyatta helped Kenya gain independence and became its first president.

In 1963, the British government left the country. Jomo Kenyatta was elected the first president of the newly formed Kenya. After he died in 1978, vice president Daniel arap Moi became president.

What type of government does Kenya have?

Kenya's form of government is a **republic**. Like the United States, the people elect many of the lawmakers to represent them.

Kenyan citizens age 18 and older elect Kenya's president and most members of the National Assembly. The president then selects a vice president and 12 members of the assembly. The president also appoints ministers to run government departments.

Fact!

From 1982 to 1991, only one political party was allowed in Kenya. Presidential elections had only one candidate. Other parties were allowed after 1991.

People from all parts of Kenya came together in 2003 to help write the country's new constitution.

Kenya is divided into seven **provinces** plus the Nairobi area. Provinces are broken down into districts. Province and district leaders are chosen by the president. Chiefs govern areas called locations within these districts. Chiefs are powerful men who are respected by the people.

What kind of housing does Kenya have?

Most Kenyans live in the countryside. Traditional houses are made of mud, twigs, and leaves. Today, many builders use stone.

The Masai people move from place to place to find food for their livestock. They build their homes quickly from sticks and mud.

Where do people live in Kenya?

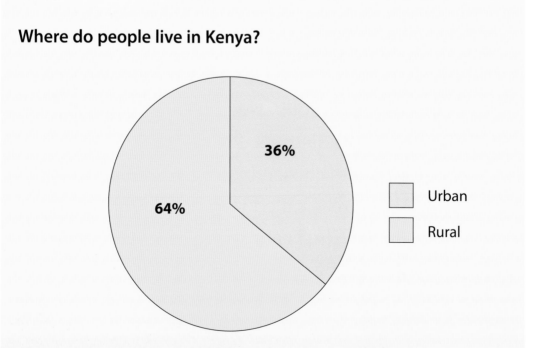

36%

64%

Urban

Rural

Stone buildings crowd together in Mombasa as new skyscrapers rise up in the distance.

About one-third of Kenyans live in the cities. Most city homes are made of stone. Outside Nairobi, poor Kenyans live in **shanty towns**. In these areas, people make homes from simple materials, such as cardboard or scrap pieces of wood.

What are Kenya's forms of transportation?

In the countryside, most Kenyans walk from place to place. Very few Kenyan roads are paved. Most Kenyans do not own a car.

In the city, most Kenyans walk or take public transportation. Buses and taxis are usually crowded. Minivans called *matatus* are popular taxis. Train travel is common between towns.

Many Kenyans have learned how to carry things a long distance by balancing them on their heads.

Mombasa is Kenya's busiest seaport.

There are over 150 small airports in Kenya. Major international airports are located in Nairobi, Eldoret, and Mombasa. Mombasa is also a major seaport along the Indian Ocean.

What are Kenya's major industries?

About 75 percent of Kenyans work in agriculture. On large farms, coffee and tea are grown to sell as exports. Small farmers grow **maize** to feed their families.

Tourism has become very important in Kenya. People come from all over the world to see Kenya's wildlife. Every morning and evening, tour groups ride into the countryside to look at the wild animals. In one day, they might see hippos, elephants, gazelles, water buffalo, and lions on the savanna.

What does Kenya import and export?	
Imports	Exports
machinery	tea
oil	coffee
motor vehicles	fish

Farmers harvest coffee beans on large plantations to sell to countries around the world.

In more urban areas, Kenyan factories make cement, paper, and beverages. These products are then sold in Kenya or to other countries.

What is school like in Kenya?

Kenyan children go to primary school from ages 6 to 14. Primary school is free in Kenya, but families must pay for uniforms and books at most schools. Some Kenyans cannot afford to buy these things. For this reason, some children never go to school.

After completing primary school, all students must take a test. If they pass, they can continue on to secondary school.

Many students in Kenya must buy school uniforms to wear in class.

Students in Nairobi play outside in their school yard.

Many schools in Kenya are simple, square buildings made of concrete. There are openings for windows, but often there is no glass. Some of these schools don't have desks. Students must sit on benches to learn the day's lessons.

What are Kenya's favorite sports and games?

Soccer is the most popular sport in Kenya. Kenya has several major soccer teams. Large crowds gather to cheer on the players. Kenyans play soccer at school, in parks, or in open fields. If there is no ball, players may kick around a bundle of rags.

Children in villages also play checkers and jacks. Students can join rugby, cricket, or volleyball teams at their schools as well.

Fact!

Kenyan runner Kip Keino was 24 years old when he competed in the 1964 Olympics. Later in life, he opened a home for children without parents.

In the 1960 and 1970s, runner Kip Keino set world records and won four Olympic medals.

Kenya has some of the fastest runners in the world. The most famous runner is Kip Keino. He competed in three different Olympics and won four medals. Two of them were gold.

What are the traditional art forms in Kenya?

Kenyan folk artists carve animals from wood and **soapstone**. They also make brightly colored pottery and baskets.

Each of Kenya's many tribes has its own music and dance. People build instruments using things from nature. They might stretch an animal skin over a hollow log to make a drum. Seeds and stones inside dry gourds turn them into rattles. Dancers might wear costumes of brightly colored cloth and animal masks carved out of wood.

Fact!

Ngugi wa Thiong'o is a famous Kenyan author. His stories about life in his country sometimes include magical happenings.

Young people in the Masai tribe learn one of the many traditional dances in Kenya.

Kenyans love to tell stories. They often combine storytelling with musical instruments and singing. Their folktales feature many local animals. Each tale passes on bits of tribal wisdom.

What holidays do people in Kenya celebrate?

Kenyans celebrate many national holidays. Jamhuri Day on December 12 marks the day that Kenya became an independent nation. People celebrate Jamhuri Day with huge feasts, dance contests, and parades. *Jamhuri* is the Swahili word for "republic."

June 1 is Madaraka Day. It celebrates Kenya's first independent government. The president gives a speech about Kenya's heroes and shares his vision for the future.

What other holidays do people in Kenya celebrate?

New Year's Day
Labor Day
Boxing Day
Kenyatta Day

Band members in Kiambu march along the streets to celebrate Jamhuri Day.

Kenyans also celebrate religious holidays. The majority of Kenyans are Christian. They celebrate Easter in spring and Christmas in winter.

Muslims in Kenya observe Ramadan. During this holiday, people fast from sunup to sundown. Ramadan ends with a feast called Eid al-Fitr.

What are the traditional foods of Kenya?

Ugali is an important part of the Kenyan diet. Maize is mixed with water to create a batter. When the batter is cooked, vegetables or meat are added.

In towns and cities, street merchants sell many kinds of food. Fruit, nuts, rice, and beans are common items. **Samosas**, peanuts, and roasted corn are popular snacks. Samosas are fried pastries filled with vegetables, spices, and sometimes meat.

Fact!

Some Kenyan ethnic groups herd cattle. These groups mix cow milk with cow blood for food.

Outdoor markets in Kenya's cities can be quite colorful places to shop for all kinds of food.

Kenyans enjoy many types of local fruits. Bananas, mangoes, pineapples, and other fruits grow well in the Kenyan soil.

Although Kenya is famous for its coffee, tea is the most common drink. Kenyans usually add sugar and milk to their hot beverages.

What is family life like in Kenya?

City life and country life are very different in Kenya. In the country, family members work on their farms. Women and girls tend crops, cook, clean, collect water, and gather firewood. Men and boys herd the livestock. Relatives often live close together.

What are the ethnic backgrounds of people in Kenya?

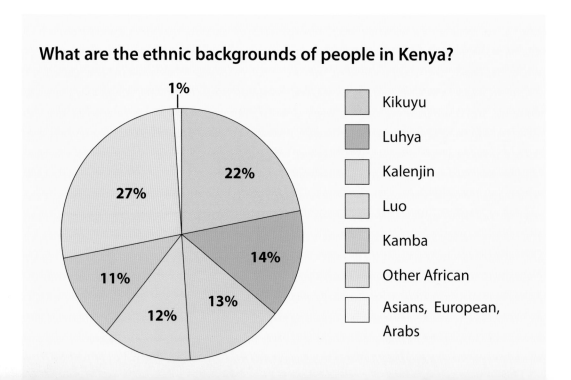

Kikuyu
Luhya
Kalenjin
Luo
Kamba
Other African
Asians, European, Arabs

Kenyan families live and work close together whenever they can, especially in the country.

In the city, family members choose from a variety of jobs. More women work outside the home. Grandparents, aunts, and uncles may live much farther apart.

While city and country life are different, one thing remains the same. All Kenyans value family loyalty. They care for each other and show great respect for their elders.

Kenya Fast Facts

Official name:

Republic of Kenya

Land area:

*224,962 square miles
(582,650 square kilometers)*

Average annual precipitation:

40 inches (100 centimeters)

Average January
temperature (Nairobi):

*77 degrees Fahrenheit
(25 degrees Celsius)*

Average July
temperature (Nairobi):

*69 degrees Fahrenheit
(20.6 degrees Celsius)*

Population:

34,707,817 people

Capital city:

Nairobi

Languages:

*English, Swahili, and many
tribal languages*

Natural resources:

*limestone, salt, gemstones,
wildlife, hydropower*

Religions:

Protestant	*45%*
Roman Catholic	*33%*
Muslim	*10%*
Other	*12%*

Money and Flag

Money:

Kenya's money is the Kenyan shilling. In 2016, one U.S. dollar equaled about 102 Kenyan shillings. One Canadian dollar equaled about 78 Kenyan shillings.

Flag:

The Kenyan flag has five bands. The bands are black, white, red, white, and green. A Maasai shield and two spears are in the middle of the flag.

Learn to Speak Swahili

Many Kenyans can speak three languages. They speak the language of their ethnic group, such as Kikuyu or Masai. Many also speak English and Swahili. Learn to speak some Swahili using the chart below.

English	Swahili	Pronunciation
hello	jambo	(JAHM-bo)
good night	lala salama	(LA-la sa-LAHM-ah)
thank you	asante	(ah-SAN-tay)
good	nzuri	(en-ZUR-I)
wait	ngoja	(en-GOH-jah)
good-bye	karibu	(kah-REE-boo)
no	hapana	(hah-PAH-nah)
yes	ndio	(en-DEE-oh)

Glossary

maize (MAYZ)—a type of corn

province (PROV-uhnss)—a district or a region of some countries

republic (ree-PUHB-lik)—a form of government headed by a president with officials elected by the people

samosa (suh-MOH-suh)—a pastry filled with spices, vegetables, and sometimes meat

savanna (suh-VAN-uh)—a flat, grassy plain found in tropical areas containing few or no trees

shanty town (SHAN-tee TOWN)—an area of a city where there are many shacks and sometimes no running water or electricity

soapstone (SOHP-stohn)—a soft stone found in Kenya

ugali (u-GAH-lee)—a common African food made of cornmeal and water

Internet Sites

FactHound offers a safe, fun way to find Internet sites related to this book. All of the sites on FactHound have been researched by our staff.

Here's how:
1. Visit *www.facthound.com*
2. Choose your grade level.
3. Type in this book ID **0736867724** for age-appropriate sites. You may also browse subjects by clicking on letters, or by clicking on pictures and words.
4. Click on the **Fetch It** button.

FactHound will fetch the best sites for you!

Read More

Auch, Alison J. *Welcome to Kenya.* Spyglass Books. Minneapolis: Compass Point Books, 2002.

Derr, Victoria, and Roseline NgCheong-Lum. *Welcome to Kenya.* Welcome to My Country. Milwaukee: Gareth Stevens, 2000.

Fontes, Justine, and Ron Fontes. *Kenya.* A to Z. New York: Children's Press, 2003.

McQuail, Lisa. *The Masai of Africa.* First Peoples. Minneapolis: Lerner, 2002.

Index